William Black

John Maclean

Contents

PREFACE. 7
I. THE BIRTH OF A MOVEMENT. 8
II. MAKING THE MAN. 14
III. THE MARITIME ITINERANT. 20
IV. THE INTREPID PIONEER. 26
V. BLACK AND WESLEY. 31
VI. PERSONAL CHARACTERISTICS. 37
VII. LAST DAYS AND AFTER. 43

WILLIAM BLACK

BY

John Maclean

PREFACE.

While there are several sketches of the life and work of the subject of this book, they are all based upon the "Memoirs of William Black" by the Rev. Matthew Richey, D. D., which was published in Halifax, Nova Scotia, in 1839. Some additional information is to be found in Dr. T. Watson Smith's History of the Methodist Church of Eastern British America. The former volume contains the interesting Journal of the famous missionary, and is therefore of great value. As it has long been out of print, and it is well-nigh impossible to secure an old copy, and as there is no likelihood of it being republished, we have deemed it commendable to publish the following pages. We have sought to condense as far as possible, giving the chief facts in his life, and to produce in popular form a volume which might be read with profit, and within the reach of all. As a study of spiritual forces and an appreciation, it might have been enlarged to considerable size, and it has been difficult indeed to keep within the limits which we had set for the volume, but that would have been to defeat our object, of writing a small book, in which the salient features of his life and work were seen, and at such a price that the poorest in the land might secure a copy. We dare not forget the work of our fathers, and we must not permit the memory of William Black to be lost in oblivion, for he builded better than he knew, and we are heirs of his work and influence, and his example is a stimulus to us all. In that spirit have these pages been written, and we hope that they will help keep alive the memory of a great and noble man, a pioneer and patriot, who gave his life for Christ and his fellow man.

JOHN MACLEAN.
WESLEYAN OFFICE,
Halifax, Nova Scotia.

I.
THE BIRTH OF A MOVEMENT.

Had Longfellow the poet extended his studies a few years later than the time of the event which formed the subject of Evangeline, he would have come in contact with another race of men, of different breed, language and faith, than that of the Acadians, who were as brave as any of those who sailed away from the valley of the Gaspereaux. For almost coincident with the expulsion of these hardy folk from the fertile fields of the Annapolis Valley, there came visitors from the New England colonies, induced by offers of land, but these were deterred from settlement on account of a fear lest freedom of religious worship should not be accorded them.

Brought up under the influence of the descendants of the Pilgrim Fathers, they prized too highly their religious liberty to barter it for lands or gold, and not until a second proclamation was issued, granting liberty of conscience and worship to all Protestants, did settlers come in large numbers. Five years after the Acadians were expelled emigrants began to arrive in considerable numbers from New England and from Great Britain and Ireland. This was the beginning of a new era, in which the principles of the Protestant Reformation were to be tested, upon soil consecrated by the faith and piety of the Roman Catholic exiles, and an opportunity was found for the expression of the new faith in the moulding of individual character.

While the province was issuing invitations for new settlers and wishing to grant concessions to sturdy and loyal folks, a great awakening was taking place in England, the influence of which was destined to become a strong factor in making a new race on the Western Continent, and to mould in a great measure the social and religious life of the people of Nova Scotia. A revival of spiritual life was in progress under the preaching of Wesley and Whitefield, which was quickening the consciences of the people, imparting high ideals and renovating the social and political life of the nation.

Methodism was doing greater things for the English speaking race than Luther among the Germans, as it infused a spirit of joy and freedom from ritual, with greater liberty of thought and action. It was an era of great names beyond the pale of the national church. The passion for souls became so intense in the hearts of many of the clergy that they gladly espoused the hated name of "Methodist," while others no less zealous stood aloof from the special movement because of its Arminian doctrines.

Whitefield, the prince of orators, stalked through the land proclaiming salvation for sinners, and not content with conquests won in the sea-girt isles, he needs must cross the ocean to tell the story of the ages to wondering thousands. John Berridge, the witty yet zealous vicar of Everton, itinerated through the country and in one year saw not less that four thousand awakened. William Grimshaw, the eccentric curate of Haworth, superintended two Methodist circuits while attending to his own parish, and Vincent Perronet, vicar of Shoreham, who was so trusted a counsellor that Charles Wesley called him the Archbishop of Methodism, gave two sons to the Methodist ministry, and besides being the author of the hymn, "All Hail the power of Jesus Name," Wesley dedicated to him the "Plain Account of the People called Methodists."

The great revival brought into greater prominence Rowland Hill, the eccentric preacher; Augustus Toplady, the author of the Hymn "Rock of Ages;" Howell Harris, the famous Welsh orator, and the Countess of Huntingdon. These and many others were brought into closer touch with the great spiritual movement, at the period when Nova Scotia was bidding for settlers, by the famous controversy on Calvinism, which was full of spleen, and has shown us how good men may retain their piety, and still say bitter and nasty things, and use gross epithets in their zeal for religious doctrines.

But Methodism, though treated as a sect composed of ignorant and illiterate folks, was not lacking in men of culture and force. It had discovered the secret of picking men from the streets and transforming them into saints and scholars, and it was successful in its efforts. It found Thomas Olivers, a drunken Welsh shoemaker, and led him on, till he became known as a great force in the pulpit, and the author of that majestic lyric, "The God of Abraham praise" and of the tune "Helmsley," sung to the hymn, "Lo, He comes with clouds descending." It laid hands upon Samuel Bradburn, the shoemaker, and developed his gifts by the grace of God, until his discourses, rich in sublimity, and pulsating with great thoughts, charmed multitudes, and his eloquence was so irresistible that Adam Clarke, the famous scholar, declared that he had never heard his equal, and could give no idea of his powers as an orator. In its ranks at this period were to be found able scholars as Joseph Benson, the commentator, Fletcher, the saintly and acute theologian of the new movement, and Thomas Walsh, whom Wesley called, "that blessed man," and of whom he said, that, he was so thoroughly acquainted with the Bible that "if he were questioned concerning any Hebrew word in the Old, or any Greek in the New Testament, he would tell after a brief pause, not only how often the one or the other occurred in the Bible, but what it meant in every place. Such a master of Biblical knowledge he says he never saw before, and never expected to see again."

There were many others possessed of great gifts and culture, whose hearts were set on fire with a passion for souls, and the revival started spiritual forces which were felt far beyond the shores of Great Britain.

Wesley was drawing near to seventy years of age, and while travelling incessantly, and preaching every day, he was engaged in the publication of a collected edition of his works, in thirty-two duodecimo volumes. The Calvinistic controversy was at its height, the first anniversary of Trevecca College, the pet scheme of the Countess of Huntingdon, had just been held, and Fletcher was writing his famous "Checks to Antinomianism," yet, the founder of the Methodist movement was looking for other worlds to conquer, by the preaching of the Cross.

Wesley's early associations with America as a missionary to Georgia, naturally gave him an interest in the affairs of the western continent, and Whitefield's frequent visits helped to deepen Wesley's love for the people among whom he had spent the early years of his ministry. Whitefield had crossed the ocean and visited America seven times, and his visits were seasons of great power, when thousands were converted, and when he suddenly died at Newburyport, there passed from earth one of the greatest pulpit orators and evangelists in the history of the Christian Church. His death was an invitation to renewed efforts for the evangelization of America. The Countess of Huntingdon and her ministers organized a missionary band, which labored with much success in Savannah and the surrounding country, especially among the African population.

Methodism was neither silent nor powerless in sharing in the progress of the Gospel, and striving to evangelize the new world. While the great revival was stirring the heart of England, a small band of German "Palatines" which Methodism had redeemed from demoralization in Ireland, emigrated to New York, among whom was Philip Embury, and these were followed by Barbara Heck and her friends, through whose efforts Methodism found a secure place in America. The new movement received an impetus from the preaching of Captain Webb, and a call for preachers was sent to Wesley, with the result that Richard Boardman and Joseph Pilmoor were sent. Later Francis Asbury, the faithful preacher and administrator, followed, and Methodism became a church. Meanwhile Lawrence Coughlan had found his way to Newfoundland, and laid foundations upon which others built.

Bermuda had been visited by Whitefield, and in the general awakening it could not be expected that Nova Scotia and New Brunswick and Prince Edward Island would be forgotten. It was a period of emigration and revival, and in the great commotion, the present Maritime Provinces of Canada shared in the blessings of the new movement.

During the period of emigration to Nova Scotia, four different parties came from Yorkshire, England, the first arriving in 1772. It was natural to expect, that coming from a district, memorable as the scene of many visits from the Wesleys, a bit of land consecrated with the tears and labors of John Nelson, the stalwart hero, and kept fresh with the hallowed memories of the saintly Hester Ann Rogers, there should be among the emigrants many who were loyal and devoted Methodists. Yorkshire Methodism was of that strenuous type which must give expression to its faith in hearty song, and lively preaching, and these sturdy settlers were an acquisition to the province, which the politicians were sufficiently alert to see, could not fail to supply the elements of stability and growth.

The majority of these people settled in the county of Cumberland, and began life anew, with intense loyalty to the institutions, and high ideals. The province had not fully recovered from the effect of the spirit of disloyalty which culminated in the expulsion of the Acadians, although there followed a period of peace, but despite the efforts of the Government in making roads, and instituting public works, the settlements were sparse, and the Indian was still in the land. There was only one minister in the county, the Rev. John Eagleson, who had been sent out in 1769 by the Society for the Propagation of the Gospel, while in the province there were a few Anglican, Congregational, Presbyterian and one Baptist church, but places for holding religious worship were few and far between, and the first Methodists consequently began prayer meetings in their homes, and through them souls were led to Christ. Whatever religious services were held they attended, and thus kept alive the glowing embers of their faith and zeal.

An incipient rebellion, induced by the Revolutionary war, and maintained by the sympathy of the colonists who had revolted in New England, unsettled the minds of the people, and made it dangerous for them to attend religious worship, and consequently the cause of religion suffered, and many forsook the faith of their fathers. A few still remained true, and amid many discouragements prayed for the dawn of a new day.

Without any propagandist effort, Methodism was spreading. Spontaneously it had gone out over Great Britain and Ireland, and into what is now the United States, to the West Indies, and Nova Scotia, but the time was ripe for complete organization as a missionary church. The time had come and with it the man in the person of Thomas Coke. While Nova Scotia and the American colonies were suffering from the Revolution, Wesley and Coke had met for the first time, and thus began a union which made Methodism a great missionary organization. The man for America had not yet come to the fullness of his power, but Francis Asbury was reaching out and getting ready to become essentially the founder of Methodism in the United States. The man for Nova Scotia had not yet arrived, as he was only a stripling at his father's home in Amherst, and was still a stranger to the grace of God.

The introduction of Methodism into Nova Scotia was not the establishment of a sect or a party in dogmatic theology, but it was the revival of spiritual Christianity, exempt from the trammels of ecclesiasticism and the exclusiveness of dogmatism. As such it became a strong and elevating factor in the social life of the people, imparting lofty ideals, which were wrought out in moral strength, making loyal citizens and men and women of power and gentleness.

There was something lacking to secure unity and strength in the scattered forces of the new movement. Prayer meetings and preaching services were held, and souls were won to the faith, still there was no organization and there could not be until a leader should come forth, who would command by his genius and concentrated effort unity of administration.

Though not the original founder of Methodism in Eastern British America, the man who in the providence of God was destined to unite the scattered forces and to give birth to the new movement, and who, by his intrepid spirit and enthusiastic and incessant labours as a great evangelist, was to spread the doctrines which were so full of power in the revival in England, throughout that portion of territory now known as the Maritime Provinces, was William Black, a man of faith and power, whose memory is revered by thousands, and whose descendants still abide with us.

II.
MAKING THE MAN.

William Black was well born. The time was auspicious. The date of his birth is 1760, and with that date as a centre, despite the fact that the tone of public morality was low, there are names belonging to the period which suggest genius and influence. Edward Young had just published his "Night Thoughts," Thomson, the poet and author of "The Seasons," and Isaac Watts had just passed away, Lord Littleton had written "The Conversion of St. Paul," Gray's "Elegy in a Country Churchyard" was being eagerly read by the people, Blackstone's famous "Commentaries on the Laws of England," had made a profound impression, Johnson had completed his "Dictionary" and Oliver Goldsmith was writing his immortal works. There were others who were in the heat of the literary battle. This period saw the beginning of the modern novel in the writings of Richardson, Fielding and Smollett, then too was published Adam Smith's "Wealth of Nations," Hume's "History of England," and Gibbon's "Decline and Fall of the Roman Empire." The two great literary frauds in our language were then given to the world in Chatterton's "Poems," and Macpherson's "Ossian." It was the age of Pitt and Burke, and Fox, of Horace Walpole and Chesterfield in English politics, Benjamin Franklin was then a potent force in America, Butler and Paley and Warburton, and Jonathan Edwards and Doddridge with many other equally powerful names were moulding the theology of the age.

Greater than any of these, however, were the Wesleys and Whitefield, as they raised both sides of the Atlantic to new ideals, and stirred the nation to a larger and deeper life.

William Black came into the world at a time when great events were being done, and though he was still young when he left the land of his birth, the silent and unseen forces which work upon men's minds and souls could not be without their influence upon him.

He was born at Huddersfield, in the West Riding of Yorkshire, England, an important market town, beautifully situated on a slope of a hill in the valley of the Colne, fifteen miles distant from Bradford, and a little over sixteen from Leeds. It was a place of considerable antiquity, being mentioned in Domesday, but its chief importance dates from the establishment of the woolen industry, being now the principal seat of the fancy woolen trade in England. Kirlees Park, three miles from the town, is popularly supposed to be the burial place of the famous Robin Hood.

When William Black was only five years old John Wesley preached to a large congregation in the Rev. Henry Venn's Church in the town. This man of God was a zealous Methodist Churchman, who made Huddersfield the headquarters of extensive labors in all the neighboring region, sympathizing with the great Methodist revival, accompanying Whitefield on evangelistic tours, and for more than thirty years, he co-operated with the Wesleys and other workers in many parts of England and Wales. Though still retaining his connection with the Church of England, he continued in labors abundant, preaching in private houses, barns and in the open air, until old age. His son, the Rev. John Venn, became the projector of the Church Missionary Society. Methodism was firmly established in Huddersfield, and its influences were not unknown to the Black family. In 1767, one fourth of the members of the Methodist Church in the United Kingdom were in Yorkshire, and among the first settlers who came to Nova Scotia were some who were identified with that church, and had listened to Wesley and his preachers.

William Black, the father of the future pioneer and evangelist, was born in 1727, in Paisley, Scotland, a large manufacturing town noted for its shawls, great preachers, and the birthplace of Tannahill, the poet. He came of an independent family, as learned from the fact that his father kept a pack of hounds, and spent his leisure in the chase. When he attained his majority he became a traveller for a large industry, which necessitated some journeys to England, and there he met his future wife, and made his home in Huddersfield. The spell of Scottish literature must have fallen upon the young man, for Robert Burns, the poet, was then at the height of his fame, Alexander Wilson, a native of Paisley, had not yet won his place as a poet, though he too, emigrated to America, and became the pioneer and founder of American Ornithology, but there were other writers whose impress must have been felt by the Scotch youth.

In Elizabeth Stocks he found a lady of refinement and wealth, and the future missionary a good Christian mother. She had been converted at sixteen years of age, and her influence upon the home, and especially upon the lad was elevating, and destined to leave its mark upon the future. The father, with Scotch shrewdness, made a visit to Nova Scotia to spy out the land before removing his family from their English home. The mother watched tenderly over all the members of the family, but William, the second oldest, seemed to call for special care, and her tears and prayers found full fruition in after years, when she had passed to her reward. Frequently did she relate to her son William the story of her conversion, and with tears besought him to serve God. Alone she prayed with him, and pressed home upon his conscience the necessity of being born again. Surely this child was born well, and his future was not all of his own making.

He must have been a precocious child, or else his religious sensitiveness must have been induced by his mother's teaching, influenced by the great doctrines of the Methodist revival. We are not now accustomed to hear a child of six years of age, bewailing his lost state in language suggestive of Bunyan's condition, when he was under deep conviction of sin. He tells us that when he was five years old he had some serious impressions, and God's Spirit began to operate upon his mind, and when he was six, he often wished that he was a toad or a serpent, because they had no soul, and were not in danger of being lost forever. Again he says, that many times before he was ten years old, he "would have overturned God's government and dethroned the gracious Author of my being." He enumerates his early vices and lashes his soul in despair. Such religious sentiments in one so young seem to mark him as one who had in his soul the elements of a monk, and we should not have been surprised had he become a zealous disciple of Saint Francis of Assisi.

Like John Wesley, whose escape from perishing in the burning of the Epworth parsonage is noted as a remarkable providence, William Black had a narrow escape from drowning in a large trough when a child, and this circumstance made a lasting and favorable impression on his mind. In his mature years he recalled the event with gratitude to God.

Several years of his childhood were spent with his maternal uncle, Mr. Thomas

Stocks, at Otley, where he was placed at school. There he remained until he was about thirteen years of age, when the disciplinary rules of the school, and very likely a severe castigation, so annoyed him, that he left his uncle's care and returned to his father's home. His father was at that time making preparations for his voyage to Nova Scotia, and deemed it prudent to allow the lad to remain with his mother, though he had decided objections to his apparent ingratitude and stubbornness, in leaving the home of his uncle. Under the influence of his mother's teaching and prayers, his religious impressions were deepened, but the jests of his companions at school made him stifle his convictions, and continue his career of youthful carelessness and sin.

In April 1775, the whole family, consisting of the father and mother, with four sons and one daughter, sailed from Hull, and after a prosperous voyage arrived at Halifax, Nova Scotia, where they remained a fortnight, proceeding afterward to Cumberland, which they reached in June. A serious blow fell upon the family in their new home, by the death of Mrs. Black, about a year after they had settled in the province, she having been seriously injured when boarding the vessel at Hull. Unfortunately for the lad of sixteen, so sadly bereft of his good mother's care and influence, he was thrown among gay companions, who in a new country gave free rein to their passions, in wild orgies by day and night. His evenings were spent in dancing and playing cards, yet amidst the frivolity he was unhappy, and he betook himself to prayer, that he might be able to break the chain of evil habits.

For three years this condition of affairs existed, and the spirit of unrest increased, with discord in the family, but the dawn of a better day was close at hand. There were several in the neighborhood who enjoy the honor of being the first Methodists in Canada, among whom were the families of Dixon, Wells, Trueman, Fawcett, Newton, Scurr, Chapman, Oxley, Donkin, Dobson and Weldon, whose descendants, with those of the Black family, remain with us till the present day.

Through the zealous labors of these families in class meetings and prayer meetings, there was a great revival in the spring of 1779, which stirred the whole neighborhood. Among those who were awakened and soundly converted, were all the members of the Black family. William was then nineteen years of age, and shortly afterward he wrote an account of his conversion to John Wesley, who introduced it in his journal, under date of April 15th, 1782.

The story of his spiritual struggles, his prayers for release from the burden of sin, and the great joy he experienced when light came to his soul, form a charming bit of biography. The change in his own life was thorough, the home was transformed by the conversion of every member of the family, and though he subsequently experienced doubts and temptations, he gradually grew in grace, being confirmed in the faith, until the Sabbath became a market-day in his soul.

Like every new convert he became anxious for the spiritual welfare of his fellow men, and first of all he became solicitous for the salvation of those in his own home. His father having married again, and all the members of the family being strangers to the joy of the forgiveness of sins, his first care was for their salvation. On the Sunday that he found peace, he spoke to his brothers one by one, waking them from sleep, and they too, were led into the light. Then he roused his father and stepmother, and they besought him to pray for them, and peace came to their souls. And the climax was reached, when next day his sister found the Lord. Thus the whole family through his exhortations and prayers, became earnest followers of Christ. Along with the joy of seeing all at home possessors of the joy of forgiveness, he set up the family altar, and then became anxious for the souls of his neighbors. As he passed them on the road he lifted his heart in prayer for their conversion, in company, he seized the opportunity of denouncing sin, much to the annoyance of some, but ultimately with spiritual profit. His early efforts at winning souls were so richly blessed, that he seized every opportunity of speaking of the good things of Christ.

In the summer of 1780, at a Quarterly Meeting held at Mr. Trueman's, he received so great a blessing that he wept, and the same evening at Fort Lawrence he made his first attempt at exhortation. From that hour he exhorted or prayed at every meeting, and though his knees trembled with fear, his tongue was loosened, and he spoke with much liberty. During the following winter he was invited to Tantramar to hold meetings, and had great joy in seeing many led to Christ. Assisted by some of the old class leaders and local preachers, he travelled over the country, exhorting as often as his duties on the farm would permit.

His first attempt at preaching from a text was in the spring of 1781, when he visited a settlement on the Petitcodiac River, and the word was with power. With so many tokens of the divine favor, it was evident that he was a marked man, and though not quite twenty-one years of age, and without any special training, he was being literally thrust out, and seemed destined to be the man who should lead the forces, and lay the foundations of Methodism, far beyond the limits of his own neighborhood. The man possessed of gifts and grace, in whom the people had confidence, and who was singularly blessed in winning souls had come, and the stripling on the farm was called to leave the plough and go forth, to proclaim the great truths of the Gospel of Christ. He was truly a chosen vessel, and fitted for a great work.

III.
THE MARITIME ITINERANT.

The population of Nova Scotia in 1781 numbered twelve thousand, of whom there were about one hundred Acadian families, and exclusive of Cape Breton, three hundred warriors of the Micmac, and one hundred and forty of the Malicete tribes of Indians. Places of worship were few and widely scattered over a large extent of country, and so destitute were the people of religious privileges that many of them seldom heard a sermon, and as some of these people had been brought up in the bonds of the faith, they naturally felt very keenly their condition.

These facts could not fail to impress very deeply such a sensitive soul, rejoicing in his first love, and possessed of a burning passion for the salvation of men, whose lips had been touched with holy fire. When his labors had been so richly blessed in the conversion of many souls, while preaching in the time spared from his labor on the farm, his mind was led toward a complete consecration to the work of a Christian minister, and when he had arrived at the age of twenty-one years, he dedicated himself wholly to the cause of Christ, as the first Methodist missionary in the Maritime Provinces. Without any college training, or the help of any minister or church institution, he left his father's home on November 10th, 1781, and commenced a career of undaunted energy, and boundless influence, laying foundations for others, and becoming essentially the founder of Methodism in Eastern British America.

During the eight years of his life from 1781 to 1789, he passed from the position of a raw youth, entering alone amid great difficulties upon the work of a pioneer evangelist, to that of Superintendent of the Methodist Church in Nova Scotia, New Brunswick, Prince Edward Island, and Newfoundland. With the zeal of an apostle he entered upon a career of usefulness, which for courage and incessant travelling and preaching, place him side by side with John Wesley and Francis Asbury. Here and there, all over the province he went proclaiming the message of salvation, preaching every day, and sometimes more frequently, as we learn of him preaching eighteen times in eight days, and upon another journey which occupied eighteen days, he preached twenty-four times.

He travelled on snow-shoes in the winter, and by boat or on horseback in the summer, and when these failed, he journeyed by log canoe, or walked over the bad roads. Once he walked forty five miles that he might spend the Sabbath with the people in Windsor. Sometimes he was in dangers by the sea, and glad after a hard day's work in the winter to have a little straw to lie upon, and a thin cover to shelter him from the cold. Like the early preachers he was often compelled to suffer opposition, rough fellows disturbing the services by shouting and seeking to break up the meeting, and some who were possessed of education demanding his authority for preaching the gospel, but to them all, he was patient, and some of his revilers were soundly converted, and learned to revere him as a man of God.

As a preacher he was eminently successful in awakening the people from a state of spiritual torpor, and winning many souls for Christ. In nearly every service there were conversions, and deep manifestations of the presence and power of God. When he preached at Memramcook, "some were deeply affected;" at French village, he left the people in tears, and the truth had a softening power upon the hearts of the people; and when he was leaving them, "weeping was upon every hand," and they pressed him so hard, that he remained another day, when many were deeply affected, and he left them in tears. On the same day and the one following, he was at Hillsborough, when "it was a moving time, many were in great distress, as appeared from their heaving breasts and weeping eyes;" at Tantramar, "many were remarkably happy," and one little girl of seven or eight years of age, "got up on a form, and told in a wonderful manner, what Jesus had done for her soul," and in this journey of eight days he preached eighteen times, and excepting two meetings, he says, "I know not a single occasion in which it was not evident that many who heard the Word were melted into tears, if they did not cry aloud for mercy."

All through his journal, there are evidences that he was a preacher of great power, eminent in the conversion of the people, for the pages abound with references to the services as "a time of power," where "many were in sore distress" as they hung around him, "eager to catch every word," and "weeping was on every hand," as they besought him to remain longer with them. When preaching one evening a young man trembled exceedingly, and cried out in agony of soul, and about bed-time, the preacher heard him praying and crying in the barn. On one of his missionary tours there were so great manifestations of power, that at Horton many cried for mercy, and others rejoiced and shouted aloud; at Cornwallis the arrows of conviction were felt by some "as they had never felt them before, and wept aloud most of the time;" and at Falmouth, "many felt the power of the word," and rejoiced exceedingly.

There were many notable conversions under his preaching. At Petitcodiac a lady whose sons had been converted looked upon him as a deceiver and opposed his work. "She wrung her hands in great distress, and cried 'O that Black! that Black! he has ruined my sons! He has ruined my sons!'" But she too found peace to her soul, after some days of deep conviction. At Horton a lady who had opposed the work of grace, was laid upon a bed of affliction, and she became so greatly agitated that for three weeks she could hardly sleep, but when William Black was praying with her, she burst forth into transports of joy in finding Christ precious to her soul, shouting, "the Lord has delivered me! O I am happy! I am happy!" All through the pages of his journal there abound remarkable accounts of striking conversions, and of people being stricken down by the power of God.

Churches were organized at the places he visited, nearly eighty persons being enrolled during one visit to Hillsborough and Petitcodiac. There wore notable revivals at Windsor, Cornwallis, Granville, Horton, Liverpool and other places. The most difficult part of his extensive field was at Halifax, where wickedness abounded, and the opposition was so great that at one time, when he was on his way to the city, his friends tried to persuade him to delay his visit, as they feared the press gang, but he went boldly forward, and preached with power.

During his labours he was not forgetful of the needs of the coloured people, who flocked to hear him preach, and many of them were soundly converted. In 1784, he preached to about two hundred of them at Birchtown, and during the year upwards of sixty of them found peace with God. Of two hundred members at Shelburne and Birchtown, there were only twenty white people, and at Birchtown alone, there were fourteen classes in a prosperous condition. At Digby in the following year, there were sixty-six coloured people members of our church.

A study of the topics and texts of his sermons shows that he preached the old doctrines, from familiar texts, easy to be grasped by the people, and he laid special emphasis always upon sin, the need of regeneration, and repentance and faith, and as he pressed home these great truths upon the souls of his hearers, there was seldom a service at which conversions did not take place. Like many other faithful ministers, he was often compelled to mourn on account of the backsliding of the people. These were seasons of depression, when he became subject to severe temptation, and mourned the leanness of his own soul. The beginning of every year however, was a time of refreshing, as he regularly and solemnly made the renewal of his covenant with God.

Despite the fact that the whole province of Nova Scotia and part of New Brunswick lay before him as a wide field of enterprise, he yearned after larger conquests, and therefore in 1784, at the earnest and repeated request of Benjamin Chappel, he paid a visit to Prince Edward Island.

He spent about a fortnight there, preaching in Charlottetown and St. Peters, with small tokens of success, and returned mourning the spiritual condition of the people.

After much thought and prayer, he was married on Feb. 17, 1784, to Miss Mary Gay, of Cumberland, an estimable woman, who had been led to Christ about two years previously under his preaching. She was possessed of gifts and grace as her letters testify, and was eminently qualified for the high duties of a minister's wife.

So extensive was the territory and so great the spiritual needs of the people that the young missionary of twenty three years of age, with a burning passion for souls, wrote to John Wesley in 1783, earnestly requesting him to send missionaries to Nova Scotia, who replied that he had hopes of sending assistance a few months later when Conference met. There being no missionaries, however, sent from Great Britain, he naturally looked towards the United States for help, and a few months after his marriage, he started for Baltimore where the Conference was to be held under the superintendence of Dr. Coke. He travelled by way of Boston and preached twice in the city, when under the first sermon one person was converted, and at the second service several were deeply convinced of sin. As he passed through New York he preached in the Methodist Church, and after the services visited a dying woman, whom he found in great distress about her spiritual condition, and he had the great joy of leading her to Christ, as she died next day, shouting, "Glory! Glory be to thy blessed name!" On his journey he preached at every opportunity and always with blessed results, and before the Conference assembled in Baltimore on December 24, 1784, he gave Dr. Coke a detailed account of the state of the work in Nova Scotia, and the Conference appointed Freeborn Garretson, and James O. Cromwell to labor in that field. Both of these ministers hastened at once to that province, but William Black spent some time in the United States preaching here and there, and called for his wife who was visiting her friends in Massachusetts, she having been born in Boston, and with the tedious travel he did not reach Halifax till the end of May. As he was returning homeward, he and his wife spent over three months in Boston, where he had the honor of laying the foundations of Methodism in that city, "the first Methodist preacher who appeared in New England after the visit of Charles Wesley," says Dr. Abel Stevens. He preached in several of the churches, removing from one to another, as the edifice became too small to accommodate the crowds who flocked to hear the young minister from Canada, until the largest church was filled to overflowing with three thousand people. A gracious revival followed this visit, and as there was no Methodist organization, the converts united with other denominations. After a period of thirty years, he preached again in the city in 1822, and many hung around the pulpit, glad to listen to the man who had led them to Christ in 1785. Six years before Jesse Lee preached under the old elm on Boston Common, William Black declared the old doctrines of Methodism, and witnessed many conversions.

With the arrival of Freeborn Garretson the work of organization was begun, as he was a leader, a man of zeal and piety, "of cordial spirit and amiable simplicity of manners, but a hero at heart," says Abel Stevens, the Methodist historian. He was a gentleman of wealth and character, who as a preacher in the United States, had been stoned, imprisoned, and his life imperilled by angry mobs with firearms, but he was dauntless in his labors for Christ. Under his preaching there were extensive revivals in the province, societies were formed and churches built. There were now five missionaries at work, Freeborn Garretson who acted as Superintendent, and made his home at Shelburne, James Oliver Cromwell at Windsor, William Black at Halifax, William Grandine, a young man who had formerly been a Methodist in the Jersey Islands, and who had just begun to preach was at Cumberland, and John Mann who came from the United States, was stationed at Barrington.

At the first District Meeting of Nova Scotia, which was held in Halifax, commencing October 10th, 1786, and lasted four days, William Black and Freeborn Garretson were appointed to the Halifax circuit, which embraced Halifax, Annapolis, Granville, Digby, Horton and Windsor, a field sufficient to tax the powers of a dozen strong men, but these were heroes in the brave days of old. Before the next District Meeting Garretson and Cromwell had returned to the United States, and their places were filled by William Jessop and Hickson. With the departure of Garretson there was lost to the province a man who was eminently fitted to lead the forces and unite them, and William Black mourned greatly that he was bereft of a friend, and a gentleman of ability and grace.

IV.
THE INTREPID PIONEER.

The mantle of Garretson fell upon Black and he was again compelled to lead the forces, and take the initiative in opening up new places and preaching at every opportunity. Aroused by the sad spiritual condition of the people, he spared not himself in excessive labors, and so successful were his efforts for the conversion of souls, that John Wesley became more concerned than ever, in the affairs in the Maritime Provinces and Newfoundland. Dr. Coke who constituted in his own person the Methodist Missionary Society, was commissioned by Wesley to visit Nova Scotia, and he embarked on September 24th, 1786, with three missionaries for Nova Scotia, but a dangerous storm which cast the vessel on the ocean for nearly two and a half months, compelled them to land at Antigua, in the West Indies, and Black was left without the promised help, as the missionaries remained there, and a new era of successful missions was begun. His field was large enough surely, for Wesley had said in a letter to him dated London, Oct. 15, 1784, "Your present parish is wide enough, namely Nova Scotia and Newfoundland. I do not advise you to go any further." During the year 1786, there was a great revival in Liverpool under John Mann, a church had been erected in Halifax in which William Black preached for the first time on Easter Sunday, and at Barrington and Horton, there were several notable conversions, still through lack of missionaries, there could not be given any assistance to Cumberland, Annapolis, Digby, and the whole Province of New Brunswick. He was however greatly encouraged by a visit to Liverpool where the revival was in progress, and by good news from River Philip, where his eldest brother John had settled as a farmer, and who had begun to exercise his gifts as a local preacher, and with so great success, that at one meeting, ten persons rejoiced in having found Christ.

At the second District meeting held on October 15th, 1787, in Halifax, there were present, William Black, William Grandine, William Jessop, and the two brothers, John and James Mann, who had come from the United States to labor as missionaries in Nova Scotia. After the third District Meeting which was held in the May following, William Black spent about a month visiting Shelburne, Barrington, Cape Negro, Port La Tour and Port Medway, and when he returned to Halifax, he was greatly encouraged by the good work which had gone on under James Mann's labors during his absence. Meanwhile, the Rev. James Wray had been sent out from England with a general charge to superintend the work, as William Black and the other missionaries had not been ordained, and could not therefore dispense the sacraments, but the relations between Wray and Black became somewhat strained, and threatened seriously to interfere with the advance of the Kingdom of God. With good judgment and much patience William Black laid the whole matter before John Wesley, but without his counsel the breach was healed, and they labored again in harmony. James Wray felt that the duties of superintending the work in the Province were too onerous for him, and he requested to be relieved of the position, and Dr. Coke appointed William Black, Superintendent of the Methodist Church in the Maritime Provinces and Newfoundland, James Wray removing to the West Indies, where he died in 1790.

The growth of Methodism was somewhat retarded by the fact that William Black had not been ordained, and consequently could not dispense the sacraments, and it was felt that his influence would greatly extend were he to assume all the responsibilities of a Christian minister. An opportunity was afforded him of being ordained, by the presence of Dr. Coke at the Conference held in Philadelphia in 1789, and accompanied by John and James Mann, who went for the same purpose, he attended the Conference, and on May 19th he was ordained a Deacon, and on the following day, an Elder. During a month spent in that city, he lost no opportunity of seeking to do good, and was cheered by learning of some being blest, among whom was a lady who had been converted under a sermon preached there by him, during his previous visit in 1784.

In a report sent to John Wesley during the year, there are shown gratifying results of the labors of the missionaries in Nova Scotia, as the church in Halifax had grown in numbers and spirituality, and throughout the Province there were about five hundred members, and with pardonable pride and joy, William Black remarks, how greatly he was comforted, as the church had grown in two years, "eight times larger, and eight times more serious and spiritual." The care of the churches pressed so heavily upon his soul, and there was so great need of additional missionaries to meet the growing demands of the wide field, that William Black hastened to Philadelphia to consult Dr. Coke, and had the pleasure of attending the Conference held in that city commencing on May 17th, 1791, at which the venerable Bishop Asbury presided. The following week, he attended the New York Conference, when six missionaries were appointed to labor in Nova Scotia. About three weeks after his return home, he went on a visit to Newfoundland, which was marked by a gracious revival, and the cause of Methodism in the ancient colony was saved.

The story of Methodism in Newfoundland, reads like a bit of romance. The first missionary Lawrence Coughlan went there in 1765, and remained seven years, amid great persecutions, being prosecuted in the highest court, an attempt made to poison him, yet not only was he able to rejoice in many conversions, but his enemies were silenced, as the Governor acquitted him, and made him a justice of the peace. His health failed, and he was compelled to return to England. His ministrations in Newfoundland however led to the founding of Methodism in the Channel Islands, as Pierre Le Sueur, a native of Jersey, during a visit to Newfoundland was deeply convinced of sin under a sermon which Coughlan preached, and when he returned to his home, spoke of the knowledge which he had received, but his friends thought him mad. When John Fentin, a recent convert, returned from Newfoundland to Jersey, Le Sueur and his wife found peace to their souls through Fentin's instructions and prayers, and a great revival commenced, which swept through the islands, and laid the foundations of religion, which have continued till the present time. After Coughlan's departure, John McGeary was sent to fill the vacancy but all that was left of the good work were a few women, and he suffered so many hardships and witnessed so little fruit of his labors that he became so despondent, as to entertain serious thoughts of abandoning the field. William Black arrived in St. John's on August 10th 1791, and spent one day in the city, during which he waited upon the Presbyterian minister, the Rev. Mr. Jones, who was a man of catholic spirit, and whose spiritual life was deep and genuine. The next day he went to Carbonear, where John McGeary was stationed, whom he found "weeping before the Lord over my lonely situation and the darkness of the people," and when he began to preach, a great revival followed, and Methodism in the colony was saved from disaster.

The power of God fell upon the people at the very first service, and many were deeply convinced of sin at every meeting. At Carbonear the people cried aloud for mercy, so that he had to stop preaching, and betook himself to prayer, when the sound of his voice was nearly drowned by the people weeping, and he came down from the pulpit and passed up and down through the church, exhorting and directing them, as many as three and four persons being in an agony of spirit in every pew. Even after the service closed, the cries and groans of anxious persons could be heard at a considerable distance up and down the harbour. At Harbor Grace, Port a Grave, Bay Roberts and other places, similar scenes were witnessed, of deep conviction for sin, and many rejoicing in the knowledge of sins forgiven. At Conception Bay during a short time spent there, two hundred souls were converted, but that was not all, for throughout the colony, William Black marched in triumph, and saw very many souls won for Christ. It is no wonder that he considered this visit to Newfoundland, as "the most useful and interesting portion of his missionary life." The Rev. Richard Knight, who spent seventeen years in the colony says, that he "organized Methodism, settled the mission property, and secured it to the Connexion, increased and inspired the society, and obtained for them the help they needed." Such a messenger could not fail to leave a deep and abiding impression upon the hearts of the people, and his departure was pathetic, as he stood for nearly an hour shaking hands with them, and at last as he tore himself away, he says, that he "left them weeping as for an only son." He secured fresh laborers from Wesley to carry on the work, and Methodism in Newfoundland was established upon a firm basis, and has continued vigorous till the present day.

Upon his arrival in Halifax he found that the gentleman who owned the church property in the city, had severed his connection with the society, and become a bitter opponent, but William Black though sorely tried, was in no wise daunted, and immediately he started a subscription list, and secured prompt and efficient help, so as to proceed with the building of a new church. One hundred pounds were raised in one day, and the society took fresh courage, and grew in numbers and strength. Having set matters in order in the city he visited Horton, Granville, Annapolis and Digby on his way to St. John, New Brunswick, where Abraham John Bishop was stationed, who arrived there in September 1791, and a week later organized the first class meeting in the city. Previous to that time several Methodist ministers had visited the then growing town, through the earnest solicitations of Stephen Humbert, a United Empire Loyalist, who landed there on May 18th, 1783. He was a New Jersey Methodist and desirous of having a society formed there. William Black arrived in November, 1791, and at once began to preach, but having seen some shipbuilders at work on the Sabbath, he denounced their action in a sermon on the same evening. A provincial statute existed forbidding anyone from exercising the functions of the ministry without a license from the Governor, and this was used to silence the courageous preacher. Undeterred by this opposition, and hindered from preaching, he spent his time visiting from house to house with blessed results. Three months later he visited St. John with permission to preach, and found a gracious revival in progress, then going to Fredericton he met a class of twenty-two, most of whom were soldiers, and during the few days spent there several conversions took place. On his return journey he visited St. Stephens, where Duncan McColl was the missionary, and he rejoiced in the evidences of growth, under the faithful labours of that devoted man of God, and this notable tour, closed with a farewell service in May to Abraham John Bishop. It was a touching scene, the people being much distressed at losing the young missionary, and well might they grieve, for after one year spent in Sheffield, he went to the West Indies to labor among the colored people and died at Grenada the following year. And thus passed away one who was esteemed as an eminently holy man, and William Black was bathed in tears.

V.
BLACK AND WESLEY.

A memorable year for Methodism and William Black was 1791, as on the second day of March of that year John Wesley passed away at City Road, London, surrounded by preachers and friends. Eight years before the young minister in Nova Scotia wrote to the aged man of God entreating him to send out Missionaries, and also expressing his desire to spend a year or two at Kingswood School, and the correspondence then begun was continued until death. With the familiarity of an old man toward a youth, William Black poured out his heart in his letters to his venerable leader, who in turn gave him counsel in his difficulties, sent him books, and treated him as a son, closing his letters with "My Dear Billy." There would be a place for him in Kingswood School, but he was not urged to attend, as Wesley laid greater stress on piety than learning, and Nova Scotia could not well spare, not even for a year or two, such a brave and intrepid soul as William Black.

It was natural that the intercourse should exert a strong and abiding influence upon the mind and heart of the missionary, who sent reports of his work, sought advice amid the difficulties which confronted him, and spoke of his spiritual yearnings with the familiarity of a little child with its parent. John Wesley became the model upon which William Black formed his habits and character, and he succeeded well, in a country with greater privations and more difficulties in travelling than in old England. Like the great itinerant, he rose early in all seasons, preached every day, as often as time and distance allowed, kept a journal in which were recorded the notable events that happened in his work, or person, and as he rode over the rough roads, the broad sky became his study where he read many volumes every year. These were not done through any servile imitation, but because of an admiration and unconscious hero worship which compelled him to follow where he admired. Wesley was to William Black a saint, an ecclesiastical statesman, an acute and learned theologian, a great winner of souls, and above all a personal friend, and when he died his loss was greater than he cared to express.

With the passing of the Founder of Methodism, there were grave fears of disagreement among the preachers throughout the Connexion, and William Black shared in the general feeling, but Dr. Coke gave him peace, in his account of the harmony of the Conference following Wesley's death.

At the Conference held in Baltimore in November of the following year, several preachers were secured for Nova Scotia and Newfoundland, and William Black who had gone to the Conference, for the purpose of meeting Dr. Coke, was induced at the doctor's request to take charge of the missions in the West India Islands, in succession to Mr. Harper, who was elected Presiding Elder of Nova Scotia, New Brunswick, and Newfoundland. Leaving his family behind, William Black accompanied Dr. Coke to the West Indies, visiting the islands, where they found wickedness and bigotry so rampant that one of the Methodist missionaries was in prison for preaching before he had resided there twelve months, and in some other places the society had dwindled on account of terrible persecution.

The climate of the West Indies was so severe upon his nervous system that William Black had serious doubts as to his duty in remaining in the tropical clime, however he was induced by Dr. Coke to become Presiding Elder of the Leeward Islands and to reside at St. Kitts. After visiting the sphere of his labors and meeting the ministers at the Conference at Antigua, of whom there were thirteen present, he returned to Nova Scotia for his family. During this visit to the Province he found that the cause at Liverpool was in such a prosperous state, that there was great need of a place of worship, and with his accustomed zeal and determination, he started a subscription list and in a few days secured three hundred pounds. His return to the West Indies with his family was signalized by strenuous efforts for the salvation of the people, but his stay was destined to be short, as Dr. Coke became convinced that owing to changes in the Islands, and the importance of the work in Nova Scotia, it was necessary for William Black to take charge of his old field. Accordingly he was recalled after spending one year as Presiding Elder in the West Indies, and singular to relate, upon the day that Dr. Coke wrote his instructions for removal, the ministers were assembled in District Meeting at Windsor, and they passed a resolution asking that William Black be allowed to assume his position as General Superintendent of the Maritime Provinces and Newfoundland.

No sooner did he arrive and was reinstated among his brethren, than he threw himself with increased vigor into the work of consolidating and extending the congregations. Prince Edward Island was visited, where a cordial reception was granted him at Charlottetown, large congregations being present when he preached. At Tryon there had been a gracious revival two years previous under the ministry of William Grandine, the results of which were still apparent, the nucleus of a congregation had been formed at Charlottetown by a class led by Joshua Newton, Collector on the Island, which met at the house of Benjamin Chappel, and when William Black waited upon the Governor, Colonel Fanning, to thank him for the use of the Church, he spent an agreeable hour, conversing freely on the advantages of religion to individuals, and society in general, and the Governor closed the interview by expressing his friendship, with a promise of assistance in building a Methodist Church. Methodism had grown in the provinces during the years since it was established, so that in 1794, there were eleven hundred accredited members, not including the number of adherents who had not united with the church.

The journal in which William Black recorded his personal experiences, and gave a faithful account, though brief, of the extraordinary events which happened in his travels, the notable conversions, revival services and progress of the kingdom of God closes with the year 1794. Limited as it is in the range of its subjects, it was characteristic of the man whose sole aim was the conversion of sinners and the upbuilding of the saints. He was too busy to continue the record, and though there were many things coming under the range of his observation worthy of preservation, he was too modest to think of writing his reflections with any view to publication.

The year 1800 was spent in England, where he attended the British Wesleyan Conference which met in London, and during his visit he made a deep and lasting impression upon the hearts of many, by his zeal and modesty. He was welcomed as the founder of Methodism in British North America, and had the opportunity of meeting some of the leaders of British Methodism, especially Jabez Bunting, with whom he had several interesting and profitable conversations, and who remained till death one of his most devoted friends. In one of his letters to him while he was attending the Conference, Bunting wrote, "My letter will, at least, be accepted as an expression of that warmth of Christian affection and esteem which I shall ever feel toward you. Unworthy as I am of your friendship, I trust that a blessed eternity will confirm and perfect the attachment which my present short acquaintance with you has inspired and that, however separated on earth, we shall together spend an everlasting existence." Two years later in another letter he says, "I often recollect with pleasure the agreeable and profitable moments we spent together at Oldham and Manchester, during your last visit to England, and am thankful to God that ever I knew you on earth, because I am persuaded that through his abundant mercy in Christ Jesus, I shall hereafter know you in heaven, and there be permitted to resume and perfect that intercourse and acquaintance, which here were so transient, and so speedily suspended by separation. In the General Assembly, and Church of the First-born, I hope to meet my honoured friend again, and to mingle with his, and with those of ten thousand times ten thousand others, my everlasting Hosannas to the Lamb that was slain. Even so, Lord Jesus! I was pleased and thankful sometime ago in a Love-feast at Saddleworth, to hear the testimony of one, who was awakened under a sermon you preached at Delph, from 'Behold I stand at the door, &c.,' on the Sunday you spent there with me in April 1800. I mention this to show you, that you have some seals of your ministry in these parts of the world, and that your labours of love among us were not in vain in the Lord."

The kindness shown toward William Black during his visit to England, and the fact that he was born there, naturally induced him to entertain the idea of taking a circuit and spending his remaining years in the old land, but Dr. Coke was strongly averse to him leaving Nova Scotia where so great success had attended his labours, and his influence was unbounded. Feeling that he could not very well leave the care of the churches to others, without some provision being made for superintending them in the event of his going to live in England, he drew up a scheme of handing them over to the Methodist Episcopal Church in the United States, and wrote to Bishop Asbury on the matter. There were however political difficulties in the way, and being unable to make satisfactory provision for supplying the churches with ministers, and the danger of disaffection in the event of a war between Great Britain and the United States, he decided to remain in Nova Scotia and continue his active duties. Possessed of administrative abilities of a high order, added to the skill and zeal of an evangelist, he was a man of mark, who could not be left in charge of a single circuit, but must have a wider field. Consequently at the Conference held in Philadelphia in 1804, Dr. Coke requested him to take a station in Bermuda for three or four years, and in order to conciliate the members of the church in Halifax by the temporary removal of their pastor, the Doctor wrote them a letter, in which he said, "Mr. Black has been your apostle for above twenty years, and it is now high time that he should be an apostle elsewhere. I have no doubt that he will have a society of six hundred, or perhaps one thousand members in Bermuda in four years. He may then, if he please, return to superintend the work in Nova Scotia and New Brunswick, but it will depend upon his own choice whether he return to you, or to England, or remain at Bermuda." William Black consented to go, and went to New York, where he engaged his passage, but was prevented from reaching his destination by some persons from Bermuda who were opposed to Methodism, and were going by the same vessel, and used their influence so that the passage was cancelled. Two years later the British Wesleyan Missionary Committee requested him to become Superintendent of Missions in the West Indies, and Dr. Coke renewed his request that he assume charge in Bermuda, but he declined the appointment to the West Indies on the account of the severity of the tropical climate, though he was willing to go to Bermuda. The Nova Scotia District Meeting however intervened, and petitioned the British Conference that he might be allowed to remain Superintendent of Missions in the Maritime Provinces and Newfoundland, and there the matter ended.

Meanwhile the arduous duties of visiting the churches and preaching continued with much success, several new churches being built and numerous conversions, among whom was Colonel Bayard who commanded one of the British regiments at Halifax during the war, and afterwards settled about 30 miles from Annapolis. He had been strongly opposed to Methodism, but was led by William Black to a personal trust in Christ, and lived such a holy life that he became known as the John Fletcher of Nova Scotia. In the midst of a great revival which swept St. John, and through the District from Barrington to Liverpool, there came opposition from some preachers from Scotland, who spurned the idea of conversion, however success followed the faithful preaching of William Black and his fellow workers and many souls were led to Christ. In 1809 he was stationed in St. John, New Brunswick, where he spent two years, but his active ministry was drawing to a close.

The privations and incessant labors began to tell upon a strong constitution, so that in 1812 he was compelled to become a supernumerary, though not desisting altogether from rendering whatever service his health would permit in extending the cause that lay so near his heart. Along with the Rev. William Bennett he was delegated by the British Conference to attend the Conference in the United States, and lay before the members the question of Canadian Methodism retaining its allegiance with the British Conference, a task which was faithfully performed, though of a very delicate character.

Increasing infirmities kept him in retirement, though he managed in the spring of 1820 to pay a visit to the United States, where he preached before Congress, and the passion for souls was still burning in his soul, for the text of the sermon was, "What is a man profited, if he gain the whole world and lose his own soul?" Brave and ever resolute, he maintained his interest in the progress of the churches which he founded, and it was with a pathos born of love to his brethren, and the consciousness that his active work was done, that he wrote to the ministers at the District Meeting held in St. John in 1823, that he was unable to attend, and sent them his blessing.

This man of daring had a definite religious experience and all his preaching was with the individual in view, his sphere of labours was not large in extent of territory, but he widened it by incessant travel, without any show of rhetoric he won his way to men's hearts and that is eloquence, and he lived to move Eastern British America by translating his message in words imperishable, and lay foundations upon which others have built. He was no common man, but an empire-builder in the brave days of old.

VI.
PERSONAL CHARACTERISTICS.

A man above medium height, stout in body and well built, clad in the fashion of the Methodist preachers of the day, with a benign countenance, his face smoothly shaven, a kindly eye, a mind ever alert, a genial temperament, and strong force of character which fitted him well for his aggressive work in a new and rough country, and you have a fair likeness of William Black. Without any college education, and with no pretentions as a scholar, he was far from being deficient in education. The preacher with his saddlebags quickly learned the value of time, as he travelled incessantly, and preached every day, and we are not surprised to learn, that he formed habits of study similar to those of the circuit riders of old England. With an intensity which is often bewildering, we read of him moving with incredible swiftness from place to place, studying at every opportunity to fit himself as an able preacher of the everlasting gospel.

His letters to John Wesley and other correspondents bear the impress of a cultured mind, in the grasp of the great doctrines which were under discussion, and the nervous strength, simplicity, purity and dignity of the language in which they are couched. The saddle, the open road, and the clear sky were his permanent study, and he read with the keen instinct of a student, whose hours were limited, as he had other work to do, and he must furbish his brain, and warm his heart by contact with the masters of literature who came at his call.

He was a constant reader of Wesley's Journal and sermons. When he was travelling to the General Conference at Baltimore, he spent his time on the vessel in study, as he writes: "Most of my time since I came on board has been occupied in reading, chiefly Flavel's Treatise on the Soul, Littleton's Roman History and Knox's Essays. Lord let none of them prove improfitable!" For spiritual growth he was accustomed to read religious biography, which is an excellent study, and he found much comfort and food for serious reflection in the Lives of John Fletcher and Whitefield. But he was not forgetful of the benefits of the solid studies which are needful for the Christian minister, and he applied himself with splendid energy to the Latin and Greek languages and works on theology. Matthew Richey who was well qualified to speak on the subject, because of his own training, and his acquaintance with William Black says: "During the time of our personal acquaintance with him, he possessed a critical knowledge of the New Testament in the original, which must have been the result of many years' application. In studying the Greek Testament, Parkhurst's Lexicon was his favorite thesaurus, and he knew well to discriminate the sound learning and theology with which that inestimable work abounds, from the fancies and eccentricities both etymological and philosophical, with which they are sometimes associated." It was his custom for many years to read Thomas a Kempis Imitation of Christ at family prayer in the Latin tongue, his wife reading the translation while he followed her in the original, and Matthew Richey adds that while he "carefully studied the Greek Testament, he was not forgetful of the Latin language, in which his attainments were very respectable." We have no record of the books he read or any account of his studies, but his Journal and letters show, that he was a student all his life, reading theology, history, biography and essays in literature with an economy of time, and an alertness, which put many of us to shame. With a yearning after wider culture he longed to go to Kingswood School in England, and when that became impossible, he devoted himself with greater enthusiasm to his studies, and employed John Wesley to send him books.

Although he was a model itinerant and was preaching every day, he pursued the method of training his own mind and instructing his hearers by courses on systematic theology, which is an ideal system for any minister. He writes: "In my last sixteen discourses I have taken a view of man in his primitive state, and in his fall, the consequences of his apostacy, to himself and to his posterity, the interposition of a Mediator, his offices, incarnation, life, death, resurrection, ascension into heaven, and session on the right hand of the Father. O, how wonderful is the process of redeeming love!" Living in a real world and deeply impressed with the needs of the people, he had no time to devote to any literary work, though he might have rendered some service by his pen to the cause of Christ, but modesty barred the way, and he was above everything else a pioneer evangelist. Only once did he consent to have one of his sermons published, and that was a discourse preached at Windsor, Nova Scotia, on Deut. 33:13. "He made him to suck honey out of the rock." When he preached a sermon on Bishop Asbury at the General Conference in Baltimore, and was importuned to have it published by that august body, he respectfully declined the honor.

William Black was a great Christian without any singularity or ostentation, ever bemoaning his lack of spirituality and yearning after holiness of heart and life. As he read the lives of great saints of other days, he prostrated himself before God, and craved pre-eminence in the attainment of the higher virtues of religious experience. Humility was one of the dominant factors in his life, which became a habit, through contrasting his actual acquirements in piety, with the saints held in much esteem by the Christian Church. He was extremely sensitive, and this subjected him to periods of mental depression, when he was severely tempted and almost given over to despair. Seasons of melancholy seemed to follow him all through life, especially at the beginning of the year, when he passed under review his life and work. But there were times when he renewed his covenant with God in writing, and when he was privileged to listen to some eminent preacher and mingle with his brethren, that the sky shone with a beauty which was divine, and bliss serene abode in his soul.

In one of his seasons of refreshing, when he dedicated himself anew, he writes: "O my God, I am Thine by a thousand ties, necessary, voluntary and sacred. Sanctuaries, woods, fields and other places, have been witnesses of the solemn vows and engagements I am under to Thee, and when I presumptuously violate them, they will bring in their evidence against me. O! by thy powerful grace, preserve me thine, thine forever!" He longed to be like Christ, and yet he could say: "Some appear to be alternately in raptures, and ready to sink in unbelief and despondency: filled with joy, or overwhelmed with sorrow. In general my walk (at least outwardly) has been pretty even. Through the severest exercises I have yet met with, the Lord has not suffered me to be greatly moved. I do not remember that anger ever had a place in my heart for one minute against any one, since I first knew the Lord. If I felt it rise, I looked to the Lord, and was delivered. Blessed be his Name for this! By grace I am saved: and grace shall have the glory. I am never enraptured with joy, nor overpowered with sorrow: yet neither am I without joys and sorrow. At times I feel Jesus inexpressibly precious: and at such seasons I long for holiness, for a full conformity to the divine will."

He was a man of prayer, rising early to be alone with God. Never did hunter pursue game with greater zest than he in his passion for the souls of men. His sermons had ever in view the conversion of sinners, and he often employed his pen in writing to individuals about salvation. Three of these letters addressed respectively, to Lawyer Hilton of Cornwallis, Major Crane of Horton, and James Noble Shannon of Horton, who afterwards removed to Parrsboro where he died, breathe a spirit of intense solicitude, and remind one of the writings of Richard Baxter the noble Puritan. In the letters he pleads with these gentlemen to seek salvation, and with such arguments, persuasive speech and love, that they were effective in leading them to Christ.

In conversation he was chaste in language and always spiritual. In one of his letters to his father-in-law, he pleads with him to be reconciled to God, and after pressing home the truth with fidelity without rudeness, he concludes; "This is the religion, in the propagation of which I desire to spend my life. This I recommend to my father. But I stop, perhaps I offend. I did not think of saying half so much. But this is my darling topic, and therefore I must beg you to bear with me." He was charitable towards others, though he differed with them in religious belief, and with commendable liberality, he held both ministers and people of the Anglican faith in the highest esteem, and associated with the Baptists often preaching in their churches, even going so far, though believing in the validity of sprinkling as a mode of baptism, as to baptize by immersion, those who desired that mode of having the ordinance administered. Whilst holding tenaciously the doctrines and institutions of Methodism, he loved those who were united to him by a common faith.

During the first years of William Black's evangelistic labors, when several hundreds were converted and had joined the church, he was confronted with Antinomian teaching, through several visits from Henry Alline, who resided at Falmouth, Nova Scotia. Being called of God to preach in 1776, Alline itinerated through Nova Scotia, New Brunswick, and Prince Edward Island, preaching a strange mixture of doctrines, which unsettled the people in the churches, and many withdrew and formed the denomination of New Lights or Allinites, a body which had some influence until his death at Northampton in New Hampshire, United States, on February 2nd, 1784, when it gradually declined and was absorbed by other denominations, especially the Baptists. Alline published his peculiar views in a volume, entitled "Two mites on some of the most important and most disputed points of divinity cast into the treasury for the poor and needy, and committed to the perusal of the unprejudiced and impartial reader, by Henry Alline, servant of the Lord to His churches." A reply to this book was published in a volume by the Rev. Jonathan Scott, of Yarmouth, Nova Scotia, which contains copious extracts from it. Alline misrepresented all the leading doctrines of Christianity, assailing predestination and election, maintaining the freedom of man's will and upholding the final perseverance of the saints, emphasizing strongly conversion, and that the soul is at the same moment completely sanctified, while sin remains in the body; denying the resurrection of the body, and though sometimes practising water baptism, he denied its utility. He was a man of good address, eloquent of speech and of a lively disposition, and there was no doubt of his piety, as he was a good man, and these qualities made him a successful evangelist. His rank Antinomian doctrines caused havoc among the Presbyterian, Congregational and Methodist congregations in the places visited by him, and William Black mourned the withdrawal of two hundred persons in a little over a year from connection with the Methodist Church. It was very natural that the young evangelist should consult John Wesley on the matter, but the only help he received was a package of books, including two volumes of the writings of William Law, the great mystic, and instructions not to mention Alline's name in public, only to go on his way preaching the gospel. Though much depressed by the loss of so many members from the church, he had the satisfaction of seeing some return to the old fold, and toward Henry Alline himself he entertained respect. There remained no harshness, though the blow was heavy by the breach made in the congregations, as shown by a letter which he wrote to Alline when he was sick, in which, after speaking of the souls won for God, and his joy in Alline's success, he added, "Although we differ in sentiment, let us manifest our love to each other. I always admired your gifts and graces, and affectionately loved your person, although I could never receive your peculiar opinions. But shall we on this account destroy the work of God? God forbid! May the Lord take away all bigotry, and fill us with pure, genuine, catholic love!" That was charity indeed, but Henry Alline went on his way denouncing all who did not follow him.

William Black had no fine capacity for anger, for with his soul aflame with a holy passion he saw men and women as related to eternity, and he loved them. With an iron will he laughed at danger, without any austerity he was a great saint, his ideals were lofty, and cheerfulness sat upon his lips and shone in his face, a practical mystic was he without losing his head in the clouds, in brief, he was a man, a brave soul with a woman's tenderness, who held his eyes toward the Cross.

VII.
LAST DAYS AND AFTER.

The long years of arduous labor began to tell upon a strong constitution, so that gradually the physical strength of the pioneer evangelist and missionary in the Maritime Provinces became so enfeebled, that during the last fifteen years of his life he was practically laid aside. For forty years he travelled, unhasting, unresting, swift of foot, and with an unquenching passion for souls, and the hardships of those early times left their abiding impress upon his body, though he still retained his natural vigor of mind. A journey now and then in quest of health brought cheerful patience, but his work was done, while still sixty years of age. Like another Whitefield he had worn himself out in his Master's service, yet he was content that foundations had been laid, and others might build, while he shared their joy.

He lived in stirring times, and belonged to a sect that moved the world, recreating the national conscience, without disturbing the religious world with a new heresy. In 1807 the slave trade in the British Empire was abolished, and the Methodist revival introduced a new philanthropy, which brought a fresh impulse into the nation for the reforming of the prisons, greater clemency to the penal laws, with a noble and steady attempt to better the condition of the profligate and the poor, and the first impetus toward popular education. Limited in his range of vision by distance from the great centres of civilization, and absorbed in his noble task of leading men in their quest after godliness, he still kept in touch with the larger questions which affected the nation, so far as the literature of that day permitted.

His closing years were spent in the quietness of his own home, with an occasional service suited to his failing health. With a sublime simplicity and faith in the goodness of women, he found a continual benediction in his wife, who was a lady of good judgment, possessing a cheerful spirit, and as earnest as he in her yearning after holiness of heart and life, and a burning zeal for the salvation of souls. Born in Boston, Massachusetts, where she frequently heard Whitefield preach, she came with her parents to Fort Cumberland, Nova Scotia, and settled there, when the British troops evacuated her native city, and in the summer of 1781 she was converted under the ministry of William Black. For the long period of forty-three years of married life, she was the devoted companion and helper of her husband in every good work. The training of five children devolved solely upon her, as she was left alone during the long and frequent absence of her husband on his missionary tours, yet she complained not, but counted it an honor to share the joys and sorrows of a Methodist itinerant. With the true instinct of a mother she governed her home in the fear of God. When she chastised her children, she did not forget their spiritual welfare, as it was her custom after punishment, to take them alone to a private room, and there to pray with the culprit, and seldom were these seasons unproductive of serious resolves of amendment. Her letters to her husband bear the impress of a saint, in their spirit of patience, sympathy with the erring, and quest after a better life. During a period of severe sickness in the family, when three of the children were laid low, and faint hopes were entertained for the recovery of Celia, the eldest, the faith of the parents was severely tried. While they were convalescing, the mother was attacked with a raging fever, and in her weakened condition, she was strongly tempted to doubt her acceptance with God. In her distress she mourned: "I have lived too much at ease. How could I rest without daily and lively communion with God." But the clouds burst, and she was enabled to rejoice, and praise God for all his mercies to herself and family. She was a saintly woman, active in her efforts for ameliorating the condition of the poor in the city of Halifax, during her long residence there. With her own hands she made garments for the needy, stimulated others in connection with the Female Benevolent Society, of which she was treasurer for several years, and by the sweetness and beauty of her life, helped many in the paths of righteousness and peace. During the last year and a half of her life she gradually declined in health yet she murmured not, and when the end came on August 11th, 1827, as she was surrounded by husband, children, grandchildren and friends, she bade them an affectionate farewell. The last to receive her blessing was her faithful and pious black servant, but her power of speech having gone, she raised her hands to heaven as an evidence of her faith and joy, and passed home at the age of seventy-three years. Thus lived and died one of the most beautiful spirits to be found on the pages of religious biography, gentle in manners, firm in action, with a chaste reserve, a noble type of heroic womanhood.

With the passing of his beloved companion, William Black felt keenly the vacancy in his home where ill-health kept him confined, and to ensure comfort and relieve the tedium, he was induced to marry Martha, the widow of Elisha Calkin of Liverpool, Nova Scotia, in the year 1828. This marriage was highly congenial, as the lady was possessed of an amiable disposition, and she ministered to his needs and together they enjoyed good fellowship, to his death, after which event, she returned to Liverpool, where she resided till she died.

The father of William Black walked through all the years of a long life in the ways of peace, and the son rejoiced that he had been honored in leading him to Christ. For the greater part of his life he lived on his farm at Dorchester, New Brunswick, dying there in 1820, at the age of ninety-three years. He was held in much esteem in the community being appointed in 1779, Judge of the Common Pleas, and in his old age he retained so much of his vigor, that when he was eighty-eight years old, he rode on horseback a distance of thirty miles to visit some members of his family residing at Amherst.

"The world may not like our Methodists, but the world cannot deny that they die well," wrote John Wesley, and this sentence has been transformed into the well-known maxim, "Our people die well." William Black knew the art of dying well, as he always stood on the threshold of eternity, and there was no need in his closing days to make special preparation, for with heroic gladness he had fronted the foe, all through the strenuous years, and was ever ready to cross the bar. In the autumn of 1834, the cholera was prevalent in Halifax, and he was deeply concerned for the people, though he was suffering from dropsy, and his end was near. The Rev. Richard Knight who was stationed in Halifax, and had Matthew Richey as his colleague, was with him in his last hours, and he gives an account of the closing scene. "'I trust sir,' said I, 'You now feel that Saviour to be precious whom you have so long held forth to others.' He said, 'All is well. All is peace, no fear, no doubt, let Him do as He will, He knows what is best.' I referred to his long and useful life. He said very impressively, 'Leave all that, say no more. All is well.' We joined in prayer, and his spirit was evidently very much engaged in the solemn exercise. On leaving the room I said, 'You will soon be in the glory of which you have so often spoken in the course of your long ministry.' 'I shall soon be there,' he said, 'where Christ is gone before me.' After which he sank very fast, and spoke little, and that with considerable difficulty. His last words were, 'Give my farewell blessing to your family, and to the society,' and 'God bless you. All is well.'"

Patient in life, he was triumphant in death, and though there was no exultant notes in his last testimony, his faith stood the supreme test, as he drew near the borderland. He died on September 8th, 1834, aged 74 years. The remains of Mary and William Black rest in the old graveyard at Grafton Street Methodist Church, Halifax, and near the vestry door are their tombstones and those of their children. Within the church there are marble tablets to the memory of these pioneers of the faith, who laid the foundations of Methodism in the maritime provinces, and in the Methodist Church at Amherst, Nova Scotia, there is a memorial window to the founder of Methodism in these parts.

There is a larger and more abiding memorial of the heroic figure who trudged over the country in quest of souls, and that lies in the silent influence of his life, and the permanence of his work. He was a great revivalist of the enduring kind, whose exhortations were not platitudes which spent themselves with the passing hour, but, being based on the leading doctrines of the Bible, remained as a spiritual impulse for the individual, and the church. In his History of the Methodist Church in Eastern British America, T. Watson Smith quotes a characteristic sketch of William Black and his wife.

"The personal appearance of 'Bishop' Black in his late years, says the Hon. S. L. Shannon, who remembers him well, was very prepossessing. He was of medium height, inclining to corpulency. In the street he always wore the well-known clerical hat; a black dress coat buttoned over a double-breasted vest, a white neckerchief, black small clothes and well polished Hessian boots completed his attire. When he and his good lady, who was always dressed in the neatest Quaker costume, used to take their airing in the summer with black Thomas, the bishop's well known servant, for their charioteer, they were absolutely pictures worth looking at. In the pulpit the bishop's appearance was truly apostolical. A round, rosy face, encircled with thin, white hair, a benevolent smile, and a sweet voice were most attractive.

Whenever my mind carries me back to those scenes, the vision of the apostle John in his old age addressing the church at Ephesus as his little children, comes up before me as I think of the good old man, the real father of Methodism in Halifax."

When William Black was converted and began his career as the pioneer Methodist preacher in the maritime provinces, in 1779, there was only a small company in Cumberland, Nova Scotia, who reckoned themselves followers of John Wesley, but when he died in 1834, there were in these Provinces and Newfoundland, 3 Districts, 44 circuits, about 50 ministers and local preachers, with more than 6000 members of the church. But the denomination has grown since then, until in the year 1906, there are 3 Conferences, with 332 ministers, 194 local preachers, nearly 42,000 church members, 686 Sunday Schools with over 45,000 scholars, 716 churches, and 219 parsonages valued at more than two and a half million dollars, and then add to these statistics, the value of the schools and colleges belonging to Methodism in the maritime provinces and Newfoundland, amounting to 567,000 dollars, and we may well say, "What hath God wrought?"

Let us remember that when John Wesley died, there were only 287 Methodist preachers in Great Britain and Ireland, and 511 in the whole world, and we may well ponder the significance of the growth during the last hundred years in the new country where William Black was the leader and pioneer. The movement which began with Black has run through a whole century without rest or failure, the stream of conversions has continued to flow, and the spiritual impulse has been maintained, despite many changes in manners and modes of thought. The old tradition of Methodism being an aggressive force, embodied in the apt phrase "Christianity in earnest" is still true, as it emphasizes the great spiritual forces of religion, as distinguished from ceremonial and even church organization, as the essentials of our faith ever abide within. The message of the apostle of Methodism in the Maritime Provinces was charged with great truths based upon doctrine and experience, and the power which swayed the people under his preaching, has remained as an abiding spiritual force. In Black's Journal we have a charming bit of autobiography, which reveals the inner life of a man who has become a historic figure, and yet he had no desire for fame. He was an evangelist first and last, begetting influences more abiding than the centuries, and if you would estimate his worth, and measure the value of his work, look around. He lived in a religious atmosphere of his own making with the help of God, he learned the triumphant secret of religion, and he gave a noble challenge to the world, in a heroic life for Christ. The pulse of his life beats still in the twentieth century in the Maritime Provinces of the Dominion.

www.bookjungle.com *email: sales@bookjungle.com fax: 630-214-0564 mail: Book Jungle PO Box 2226 Champaign, IL 61825*

The Codes Of Hammurabi And Moses
W. W. Davies

QTY

The discovery of the Hammurabi Code is one of the greatest achievements of archaeology, and is of paramount interest, not only to the student of the Bible, but also to all those interested in ancient history...

Religion   **ISBN:** *1-59462-338-4*   **Pages:** 132
MSRP $12.95

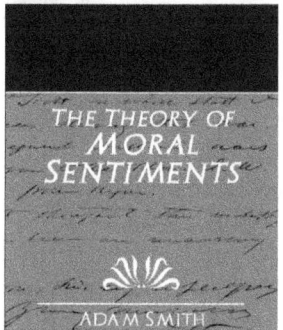

The Theory of Moral Sentiments
Adam Smith

QTY

This work from 1749. contains original theories of conscience amd moral judgment and it is the foundation for systemof morals.

Philosophy   **ISBN:** *1-59462-777-0*   **Pages:** 536
MSRP $19.95

Jessica's First Prayer
Hesba Stretton

QTY

In a screened and secluded corner of one of the many railway-bridges which span the streets of London there could be seen a few years ago, from five o'clock every morning until half past eight, a tidily set-out coffee-stall, consisting of a trestle and board, upon which stood two large tin cans, with a small fire of charcoal burning under each so as to keep the coffee boiling during the early hours of the morning when the work-people were thronging into the city on their way to their daily toil...

Childrens   **ISBN:** *1-59462-373-2*   **Pages:** 84
MSRP $9.95

My Life and Work
Henry Ford

QTY

Henry Ford revolutionized the world with his implementation of mass production for the Model T automobile. Gain valuable business insight into his life and work with his own auto-biography... "We have only started on our development of our country we have not as yet, with all our talk of wonderful progress, done more than scratch the surface. The progress has been wonderful enough but..."

Biographies/   **ISBN:** *1-59462-198-5*   **Pages:** 300
MSRP $21.95

www.bookjungle.com *email: sales@bookjungle.com fax: 630-214-0564 mail: Book Jungle PO Box 2226 Champaign, IL 61825*

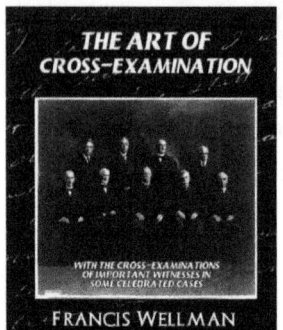

The Art of Cross-Examination
Francis Wellman

QTY

I presume it is the experience of every author, after his first book is published upon an important subject, to be almost overwhelmed with a wealth of ideas and illustrations which could readily have been included in his book, and which to his own mind, at least, seem to make a second edition inevitable. Such certainly was the case with me; and when the first edition had reached its sixth impression in five months, I rejoiced to learn that it seemed to my publishers that the book had met with a sufficiently favorable reception to justify a second and considerably enlarged edition. ..

Reference   ISBN: *1-59462-647-2*   Pages:412   MSRP *$19.95*

On the Duty of Civil Disobedience
Henry David Thoreau

QTY

Thoreau wrote his famous essay, On the Duty of Civil Disobedience, as a protest against an unjust but popular war and the immoral but popular institution of slave-owning. He did more than write—he declined to pay his taxes, and was hauled off to gaol in consequence. Who can say how much this refusal of his hastened the end of the war and of slavery ?

Law   ISBN: *1-59462-747-9*   Pages:48   MSRP *$7.45*

Dream Psychology Psychoanalysis for Beginners
Sigmund Freud

QTY

Sigmund Freud, born Sigismund Schlomo Freud (May 6, 1856 - September 23, 1939), was a Jewish-Austrian neurologist and psychiatrist who co-founded the psychoanalytic school of psychology. Freud is best known for his theories of the unconscious mind, especially involving the mechanism of repression; his redefinition of sexual desire as mobile and directed towards a wide variety of objects; and his therapeutic techniques, especially his understanding of transference in the therapeutic relationship and the presumed value of dreams as sources of insight into unconscious desires.

Psychology   ISBN: *1-59462-905-6*   Pages:196   MSRP *$15.45*

The Miracle of Right Thought
Orison Swett Marden

QTY

Believe with all of your heart that you will do what you were made to do. When the mind has once formed the habit of holding cheerful, happy, prosperous pictures, it will not be easy to form the opposite habit. It does not matter how improbable or how far away this realization may see, or how dark the prospects may be, if we visualize them as best we can, as vividly as possible, hold tenaciously to them and vigorously struggle to attain them, they will gradually become actualized, realized in the life. But a desire, a longing without endeavor, a yearning abandoned or held indifferently will vanish without realization.

Self Help   ISBN: *1-59462-644-8*   Pages:360   MSRP *$25.45*

www.bookjungle.com *email: sales@bookjungle.com fax: 630-214-0564 mail: Book Jungle PO Box 2226 Champaign, IL 61825*

QTY

☐	**The Rosicrucian Cosmo-Conception Mystic Christianity** by *Max Heindel*	ISBN: *1-59462-188-8*	**$38.95**

The Rosicrucian Cosmo-conception is not dogmatic, neither does it appeal to any other authority than the reason of the student. It is: not controversial, but is: sent forth in the, hope that it may help to clear...   *New Age/Religion Pages 646*

☐ **Abandonment To Divine Providence** by *Jean-Pierre de Caussade*   ISBN: *1-59462-228-0*   **$25.95**

"The Rev. Jean Pierre de Caussade was one of the most remarkable spiritual writers of the Society of Jesus in France in the 18th Century. His death took place at Toulouse in 1751. His works have gone through many editions and have been republished...   *Inspirational/Religion Pages 400*

☐ **Mental Chemistry** by *Charles Haanel*   ISBN: *1-59462-192-6*   **$23.95**

Mental Chemistry allows the change of material conditions by combining and appropriately utilizing the power of the mind. Much like applied chemistry creates something new and unique out of careful combinations of chemicals the mastery of mental chemistry...   *New Age Pages 354*

☐ **The Letters of Robert Browning and Elizabeth Barret Barrett 1845-1846 vol II**   ISBN: *1-59462-193-4*   **$35.95**

by *Robert Browning* and *Elizabeth Barrett*   *Biographies Pages 596*

☐ **Gleanings In Genesis (volume I)** by *Arthur W. Pink*   ISBN: *1-59462-130-6*   **$27.45**

Appropriately has Genesis been termed "the seed plot of the Bible" for in it we have, in germ form, almost all of the great doctrines which are afterwards fully developed in the books of Scripture which follow...   *Religion/Inspirational Pages 420*

☐ **The Master Key** by *L. W. de Laurence*   ISBN: *1-59462-001-6*   **$30.95**

In no branch of human knowledge has there been a more lively increase of the spirit of research during the past few years than in the study of Psychology, Concentration and Mental Discipline. The requests for authentic lessons in Thought Control, Mental Discipline and...   *New Age/Business Pages 422*

☐ **The Lesser Key Of Solomon Goetia** by *L. W. de Laurence*   ISBN: *1-59462-092-X*   **$9.95**

This translation of the first book of the "Lernegton" which is now for the first time made accessible to students of Talismanic Magic was done, after careful collation and edition, from numerous Ancient Manuscripts in Hebrew, Latin, and French...   *New Age/Occult Pages 92*

☐ **Rubaiyat Of Omar Khayyam** by *Edward Fitzgerald*   ISBN: *1-59462-332-5*   **$13.95**

Edward Fitzgerald, whom the world has already learned, in spite of his own efforts to remain within the shadow of anonymity, to look upon as one of the rarest poets of the century, was born at Bredfield, in Suffolk, on the 31st of March, 1809. He was the third son of John Purcell...   *Music Pages 172*

☐ **Ancient Law** by *Henry Maine*   ISBN: *1-59462-128-4*   **$29.95**

The chief object of the following pages is to indicate some of the earliest ideas of mankind, as they are reflected in Ancient Law, and to point out the relation of those ideas to modern thought.   *Religiom/History Pages 452*

☐ **Far-Away Stories** by *William J. Locke*   ISBN: *1-59462-129-2*   **$19.45**

"Good wine needs no bush, but a collection of mixed vintages does. And this book is just such a collection. Some of the stories I do not want to remain buried for ever in the museum files of dead magazine-numbers an author's not unpardonable vanity..."   *Fiction Pages 272*

☐ **Life of David Crockett** by *David Crockett*   ISBN: *1-59462-250-7*   **$27.45**

"Colonel David Crockett was one of the most remarkable men of the times in which he lived. Born in humble life, but gifted with a strong will, an indomitable courage, and unremitting perseverance...   *Biographies/New Age Pages 424*

☐ **Lip-Reading** by *Edward Nitchie*   ISBN: *1-59462-206-X*   **$25.95**

Edward B. Nitchie, founder of the New York School for the Hard of Hearing, now the Nitchie School of Lip-Reading, Inc, wrote "LIP-READING Principles and Practice". The development and perfecting of this meritorious work on lip-reading was an undertaking...   *How-to Pages 400*

☐ **A Handbook of Suggestive Therapeutics, Applied Hypnotism, Psychic Science**   ISBN: *1-59462-214-0*   **$24.95**

by *Henry Munro*   *Health/New Age/Health/Self-help Pages 376*

☐ **A Doll's House: and Two Other Plays** by *Henrik Ibsen*   ISBN: *1-59462-112-8*   **$19.95**

Henrik Ibsen created this classic when in revolutionary 1848 Rome. Introducing some striking concepts in playwriting for the realist genre, this play has been studied the world over.   *Fiction/Classics/Plays 308*

☐ **The Light of Asia** by *sir Edwin Arnold*   ISBN: *1-59462-204-3*   **$13.95**

In this poetic masterpiece, Edwin Arnold describes the life and teachings of Buddha. The man who was to become known as Buddha to the world was born as Prince Gautama of India but he rejected the worldly riches and abandoned the reigns of power when...   *Religion/History/Biographies Pages 170*

☐ **The Complete Works of Guy de Maupassant** by *Guy de Maupassant*   ISBN: *1-59462-157-8*   **$16.95**

"For days and days, nights and nights, I had dreamed of that first kiss which was to consecrate our engagement, and I knew not on what spot I should put my lips..."   *Fiction/Classics Pages 240*

☐ **The Art of Cross-Examination** by *Francis L. Wellman*   ISBN: *1-59462-309-0*   **$26.95**

Written by a renowned trial lawyer, Wellman imparts his experience and uses case studies to explain how to use psychology to extract desired information through questioning.   *How-to/Science/Reference Pages 408*

☐ **Answered or Unanswered?** by *Louisa Vaughan*   ISBN: *1-59462-248-5*   **$10.95**

Miracles of Faith in China   *Religion Pages 112*

☐ **The Edinburgh Lectures on Mental Science (1909)** by *Thomas*   ISBN: *1-59462-008-3*   **$11.95**

This book contains the substance of a course of lectures recently given by the writer in the Queen Street Hall, Edinburgh. Its purpose is to indicate the Natural Principles governing the relation between Mental Action and Material Conditions...   *New Age/Psychology Pages 148*

☐ **Ayesha** by *H. Rider Haggard*   ISBN: *1-59462-301-5*   **$24.95**

Verily and indeed it is the unexpected that happens! Probably if there was one person upon the earth from whom the Editor of this, and of a certain previous history, did not expect to hear again...   *Classics Pages 380*

☐ **Ayala's Angel** by *Anthony Trollope*   ISBN: *1-59462-352-X*   **$29.95**

The two girls were both pretty, but Lucy who was twenty-one who supposed to be simple and comparatively unattractive, whereas Ayala was credited, as her Bombwhat romantic name might show, with poetic charm and a taste for romance. Ayala when her father died was nineteen...   *Fiction Pages 484*

☐ **The American Commonwealth** by *James Bryce*   ISBN: *1-59462-286-8*   **$34.45**

An interpretation of American democratic political theory. It examines political mechanics and society from the perspective of Scotsman James Bryce   *Politics Pages 572*

☐ **Stories of the Pilgrims** by *Margaret P. Pumphrey*   ISBN: *1-59462-116-0*   **$17.95**

This book explores pilgrims religious oppression in England as well as their escape to Holland and eventual crossing to America on the Mayflower, and their early days in New England...   *History Pages 268*

www.bookjungle.com email: sales@bookjungle.com fax: 630-214-0564 mail: Book Jungle PO Box 2226 Champaign, IL 61825

QTY

The Fasting Cure *by Sinclair Upton* ISBN: *1-59462-222-1* **$13.95**
In the Cosmopolitan Magazine for May, 1910, and in the Contemporary Review (London) for April, 1910, I published an article dealing with my experiences in fasting. I have written a great many magazine articles, but never one which attracted so much attention... New Age/Self Help/Health Pages 164

Hebrew Astrology *by Sepharial* ISBN: *1-59462-308-2* **$13.45**
In these days of advanced thinking it is a matter of common observation that we have left many of the old landmarks behind and that we are now pressing forward to greater heights and to a wider horizon than that which represented the mind-content of our progenitors... Astrology Pages 144

Thought Vibration or The Law of Attraction in the Thought World ISBN: *1-59462-127-6* **$12.95**
by William Walker Atkinson Psychology/Religion Pages 144

Optimism *by Helen Keller* ISBN: *1-59462-108-X* **$15.95**
Helen Keller was blind, deaf, and mute since 19 months old, yet famously learned how to overcome these handicaps, communicate with the world, and spread her lectures promoting optimism. An inspiring read for everyone... Biographies/Inspirational Pages 84

Sara Crewe *by Frances Burnett* ISBN: *1-59462-360-0* **$9.45**
In the first place, Miss Minchin lived in London. Her home was a large, dull, tall one, in a large, dull square, where all the houses were alike, and all the sparrows were alike, and where all the door-knockers made the same heavy sound... Childrens/Classic Pages 88

The Autobiography of Benjamin Franklin *by Benjamin Franklin* ISBN: *1-59462-135-7* **$24.95**
The Autobiography of Benjamin Franklin has probably been more extensively read than any other American historical work, and no other book of its kind has had such ups and downs of fortune. Franklin lived for many years in England, where he was agent... Biographies/History Pages 332

Name	
Email	
Telephone	
Address	
City, State ZIP	

☐ Credit Card   ☐ Check / Money Order

Credit Card Number	
Expiration Date	
Signature	

Please Mail to: Book Jungle
PO Box 2226
Champaign, IL 61825
or Fax to: 630-214-0564

ORDERING INFORMATION
web: *www.bookjungle.com*
email: *sales@bookjungle.com*
fax: *630-214-0564*
mail: *Book Jungle PO Box 2226 Champaign, IL 61825*
or PayPal *to sales@bookjungle.com*

Please contact us for bulk discounts

DIRECT-ORDER TERMS

20% Discount if You Order Two or More Books
Free Domestic Shipping!
Accepted: Master Card, Visa, Discover, American Express

www.ingramcontent.com/pod-product-compliance
Lightning Source LLC
Chambersburg PA
CBHW081350040426
42450CB00015B/3377